Butterflies & Bruises

SAISHA

Qurate
qaratebooks.com

Butterflies & Bruises
Saisha

Published in 2025

© Published by

Qurate
qouratebooks.com

Qurate Books Pvt. Ltd.
Goa 403523, India
www.quratebooks.com
Tel: 1800-210-6527, Email: info@quratebooks.com

ISBN: 978-93-5898-718-8

to those "homes" that were simply arms
wrapped around me at my worst

Authors Note

"Butterflies & Bruises" came from a special place in my heart. That special place is actually a lot of special people in my life who took every wound I had and, instead of just bandaging it like the cliche "they healed me", they stuck butterflies on them and gave those wounds wings to fly. I don't know when those wings found shape as poetry, but I owe every word I write to the people who've loved me and who i have loved and some words (you can tell) those who've not loved me very much as well I used to think feeling so much was a bad thing- like maybe I was just a crybaby. But now, I see it as my gift. And it's a gift we all have, even if we don't always realize it. Ever heard "There's a grain of truth in every fairytale " well, there's a fragment of me in each of my poem as well. My hope is that when you read these poems, you find a piece of yourself too, however you choose to see it.

This book is as much yours as it is mine. I hope it gives you something special, whether that's comfort, understanding, or just a moment of connection. Thanks for letting me share a part of my world with you.

With love
Saisha

Contents

the art of ruin

you say you're destroyed, a force that brings despair
but oh, my love, your destruction is a treasure to share
a map-worthy journey, a path that many would choose
to get drunk on your beauty, to bask in your radiant muse

your destruction creates iridescent skies
nacreous clouds that shimmer, a beauty that never dies
you're a star that's exploded, a nebula born anew
every scar a kaleidoscope of color, a beauty shining through

why contain your supernova, your transcendent might?
why reduce your brilliance to mere ruination's sight?
you're an unfinished poem, a burdened poet's heart
even incomplete, you're art, a work that sets us apart

call yourself trapped methane, a bubble under the ice
call yourself the remains of a mythic, ancient strife
for even in destruction, your beauty brings a smile
a treasure to behold, a wonder that's worth our while.

mohobbat?

why do u look afraid he asked
well i'm afraid to open, afraid to see
the darkness that surrounds me, the uncertainty
i know life is hard, i know it's a test
but today, i can't learn, today i'm at my worst

today, i can't speak, today i'm lost
my mind a maze, my heart the cost
i'm exhausted from being strong
from being the catalyst, from moving alone
today, i broke, and i need your grace
to put the pieces back, to find my place

the "goodnight" to the rest of my nights

if I had to tell our story, I'd say the most beautiful part,
is that I found you when I wasn't even looking & now you own my heart.
if i had to study science & discoveries profound
id study how when our stars collided it shook my world around
if i had to weave dreams with threads youd be my finest lace
a tapestry of wonder where every pattern's grace
if i had to give time colours
youd be the golden hour
if my love had to grow a garden
i'd plant u as every flower
if my heartbeat had a language, a, e, i, o, u would all be 's,'
for no word can be spoken without a vowel's gentle press.
if I had to speak of something I thought would never be,
it would be the concept of "forever" and its certainty.
but if it were to be true,
i would want mine to be you.

"you exist in my world the way noone does."

only an hour

i'd been dead for an hour when he woke up alone
i'd been dead for only an hour
when my mother waited for me to come home
i'd been dead only an hour
when my so called friends had shopped for flowers
60 minutes, 3600 seconds
since my son had both his parents
but for the first time I felt free
my wandering soul felt glee
i realised I wasnt trying to hold on
i was finding a way escape all along
the thought of a happy life deceived me,
i just wanted to break free
i'd been dead for only an hour
but I'd never felt more empowered

the pinky promise that fell apart

you promised to never leave
made a bond that felt like a forever weave
our pinky fingers interlocked into one another
thinking those two words to be stronger than any other
'pinky promise' the forever that never falls apart
words swearing to be each others end, middle and start
our intertwined fingers unlocked those sacred words mocked
you left me with a hole in my heart
we couldnt even make it to the start -
you promised to stay till the day I die
I felt like taking my last breathe when you said good- bye
your fingers locked hers within two weeks
leaving me with so many answers to seek
i miss u a little harder on my silent days
and love u a little louder every way

the mask i wear

last night, I caught myself staring at the mirror
wondering if the reflection was me
or was if who was supposed to be?
covered with expectations from head to toe
i couldn't find me, it was all for show
a smile plastered on my acne-driven face
if they noticed the spots would I lose the race?.
two sizes, too big to fit into the world
clothes sown to be a perfect fit
covered from all sides, not even a single slit
i was a reflection of what the world wanted me to be was it too
late to find the real me?

lunar longing

in a star-laden sky i couldn't help but notice the moon
she was the light, the real boon
she relentlessly shone onto the land
upon the seas, mountains & sand
she had her phases, she waned & waxed
but a simple peak at her would make anyone relaxed
her subtle reflection upon violent waves
how she peered into the twilight caves
she sparkled her way through dark mists
she was beautiful despite her carved bits.
how i craved to be the moon
how i craved to be a boon

the raindrop ghosts

the water struck the ground, as if it never had before
with every rain drop, a tiny leaf had to get torn i
struck my hand out in the storm
nature was definately breaking all norms
the rain was full of ghosts that night
they were crying; missing being alive
every rain drop was shaped as a weep
emotions falling on the ground to seep.
was this a cry of help?
or just some old souls weekly welp
were those the cries of bewildered minds
or those who had answers to find
the rain was full of ghosts that night.
they were crying; missing being alive

“meant to be”

he & she were never meant to be
if he was the land
then she was the sea
every instance she found, she would push herself away
he didnt know anything else but to stay,
for him happiness was the first sip of freshly brewed tea
whereas she found home in hot midnight coffee.
for him love was a garden, only to be grown But none
of the seeds she’d sown had ever shown
she had a habit of running away.
into his arms, that was one day
but he & she were never meant to be
that was until they becamie a we
the waves of her ocean started brushing onto his rocky cusion
she pushed herself right into him
He stood right there through bright e dim
she liked her coffee hot
so he became her coffee pot
they promised to never let go
and let the garden of their love always grow

ashtray of love

you used me as your ashtray to put out the fire
then dumped me into the bay
and let every sign of us burn on a pyre
the ashes haven't even been collected yet
and you are already lighting the next match
the burns you've left all over me are hard to forget
but what stings more is how i'm still attached

the scar map

scars tender as much as timeless
every wound equal to every mess
deepness measuring the pain
a forever reminder in form of a stain
no bracelets, no sweater could hide the feeling
of being broken, of being fragile, of being human
a topography of hurt, etched on my skin, a map to my story

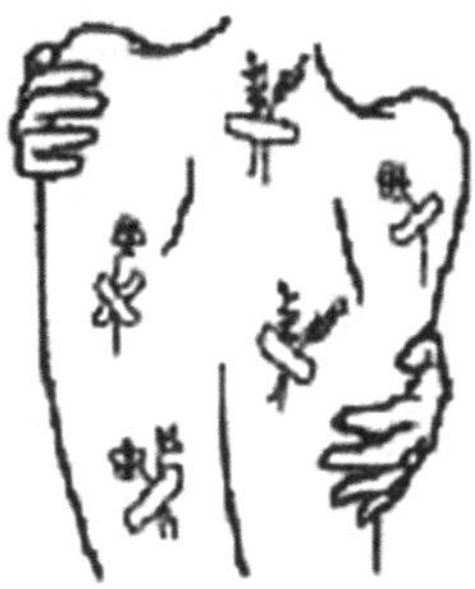

solitudes embrace

i've been worshipping solitude more and more
silence, a luxury i didn't know of before
i've been watching the dandelions dance beneath the
spotlight of the blue sky
twirling to my hearts content under the stormy night's cry
i started feeling the breeze cascade on my cheeks
stealing glimpses' of the moon, hidden behind the mountain
peak
i've been living vicariously through novels and sleeping in the
willows
passing my days, writing poems in the meadows
the world is unknown of the peace i hold in my possession of
turning all my shattered pieces into lessons
the clouds always know something i don't
the faith alone is such a marvel to behold

love at first meet?

meeting you was like falling into the bed after a long day
like smelling dandelions on a morning in may
a fresh pot of coffee on a summer afternoon
the beam between the grey clouds of the glimmering moon
all of the planets perfectly aligned
moon, stars & heaven combined
the taste of cake batter left on the bowl completion....
becoming a whole
like waking up to the song of a humming bird
like a potrait engraved with golden words

eyes that betray

i avoid looking at u because i know if i do i will be too greedy
but what can i do my eyes are needy
but looking at you comes out of habit
something inside makes me feel i wont go by without it
there's something in your drug induced smile
that makes me crave to see it all the time
they asked me whether i listened to me heart or my brain
but what happens when all my heart wants is you and
every sign of my brain is shadowed by the hearts pain
i've tried to cross borders hoping to erase every trace of you
but while running i forgot to scrub my heart clean
and now it forever bleeds for you

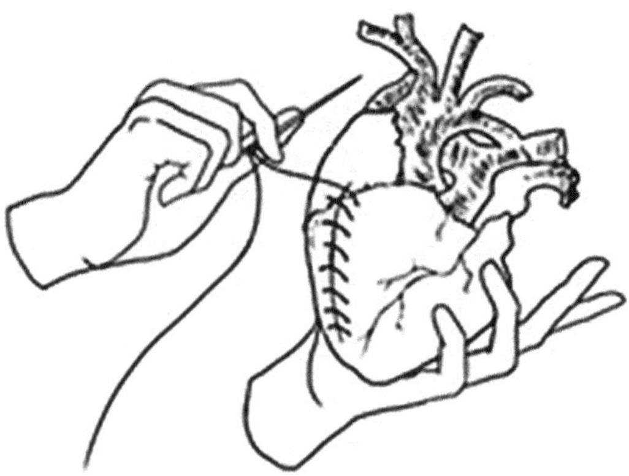

mors mihi lucrum

half timeless scars
half falling stars
dreams behind teary eyes
silent hope within loud sighs
questions that outweigh the answers filling the mind
while peace is all the heart wants to find
serotonin bursts in the veins
constantly trying to compress the pain
never enough for the eye's rain
heart as soft as that of a sage hidden behind a hard cage
half starry skies
but mostly webs of lies

unfinished pages

you didn't make it to the end of my story
but i'll always have the page folded at your part
i'll read it to wipe my fears
& i'll feel it to let out tears every instance, every sight
every i love you and every goodnight from the ending to the start
forever embroidered in my heart
i knew we were an eternity kind of memory
but i will never stop wishing for you to make it to the end of story

the naina to my bunny

she reminds me of the moon
the first sip of coffee on a sunday afternoon she was a heart healer, she made people better but who would heal the heart healer?
life forced her to fight her battles, but she stood strong against them all
she was the spring, the summer and the fall they saw her as a perfect portrait engraved in golden paint but none of that would ever come without a little restraint but little did she know
she was a green house, just beginning to grow she was smart and funny
and she was everything anyone wanted her to be you could see the stars inside her eye the moon stole peeks at beautiful smile i'm her mothers greatest fan,
because she's brought to life a world of art someone who would strengthen the beat in everyone's heart

• • • • •

someone who's voice felt like a hummingbird song like the soft warmth of the sun at dawn all the happy colors reminded me of her smile she isn't just another character in a story she's the epilogue of everything that ends with glory she reminds me of my favorite books, every of the underlined quote she has become

she gives heart thinking it would be broken, but this is a myth from which i want her to be woken because she is the stars, all the planets perfectly aligned all of heaven combined

she was the freshness of daisies freshly watered the white dandelions who think they are flawed only when they are the embodiment of perfection her beauty and character was a god sent selection her name itself makes me feel this comfort, all i wanted to tell her was honey you remind me of thy moon, first sip of coffee on a sunday afternoon

fragments of me

i'm a mosaic of everyone i loved even if it was just for a heartbeat
each shard, a memory, a piece of the past,
in my soul, their echoes forever cast. their touch, their laughter, their fleeting embrace
i still eat cake the way my grandmother taught me
too sweet by itself but perfect if dipped in the strongest tea
never forget to pout my lips because he told me it makes me look pretty
in every whisper of the wind, their voice does chime, in every ray of sun, their essence does shine.
their laughter echoes in the chambers of my heart, though they've departed, we're never truly apart. their presence lingers, though they may be gone, in the tapestry of my being, they live on.
each moment shared, a brushstroke divine, in this mosaic of love, forever intertwined. i'm a mosaic of everyone I've loved even those who i wasn't destined to meet

echoes in her eyes

her eyes told a story
far beyond all her achieved glory if u looked into them long
in capitals you'd be able to read every wrong but if u looked in deep
you could see the little her and all her weeps you could hear her screams
longing only for a few words to allow her to dream all she needed was an occasional, "good job"
but she was left wondering why of this she was robbed was it that hard to pat her back
instead of telling her about everything she lacked thousands of questions left across her heart
but no one to play the answering part those questions runs through her veins Which she prints into her story
with the typewriter in her brain was it that hard to add a too to every of her i love you's
to run your hands through her hair
and tell her all her pain would be shared? a simple sentence or even a few words
isn't reassurance something everyone is worth?

inky footprints

i have a bookshelf for a heart embedded in it every story every
part ink flows through my veins
written in it every incident with typewriter in my brain the
happiness, anger, sadness and pain
there's books i'm scared to open and some that aren't closed
stories of everyone i've ever met stretched out in endless rows
it's left inky footprints across my heart
of my first step, first word everything from the start
sometimes i flip through the pages
but there's a few books that will always be locked within the
cages

my birthday wish

you were every candle i blew out on 15th April every wish i
ever made, fulfilled
the silent words mumbled as i cut the ice cream topped cake
all my thoughts asleep and awake
you are every hope i'll ever have in human form

the only arms i wanna be in, middle of a thunderstorm the
penny i threw in the wishing well
the fine line separating me from hell

you didn't draw stars around my scars you healed them
you embraced them as part of my constellation turning my
pain into a map of our salvation

every dream that danced behind my closed eyes you made
real, beneath our shared skies
you are every sunrise after a sleepless night
every whispered comfort in the dim twilight the melody
that soothes my troubled mind the peace in chaos, the love i
couldn't find

● ● ● ● ●

you are the breath that fills my lungs anew the compass that guides me, steady and true

my anchor in the stormy seas
the only one who sets my heart at ease
you are the light that breaks through my dark the steady beat within my heart
every poem, every song, every story untold the love that fills my life with gold

bittersweet surrender

like a siren's call, you beckon me a sweet temptation, hard to flee
my heart, aflutter, like a bird set free
craving the sweetness of your love, a bittersweet spree

i swore off love, like a vow to abstain
but your presence draws me in, like a sweet, sweet pain my resolve crumbles, like a fragile, hollow reed
i succumb to your charm, my heart's deepest need

the ache of our past, a wound still unhealed yet, i'd surrender all, my heart's fragile shield
to taste the sweetness of your love, one moment's delight and risk the agony, the darkness of night

my heart, a battlefield, where love and pain collide where the sweetness of your love, my soul cannot divide i'm lost in your eyes, a siren's call
forever bound, to the sweetness of your love, i'll fall.

kaleidoscope of broken glass

she dropped the mirror, and her heart did sink a superstition's
curse, seven years to blink
but as she gazed upon the shattered glass she saw a
kaleidoscope of light, a new pass

hundreds of fragments, like diamonds bright reflected every
beam, and made the darkness light she gathered all the pieces,
one by one
and turned her misfortune into a dance begun

with every step, her spirit started to soar her smile illuminated
all that was before her soul came alive, like a work of art
a shimmering spectacle, a heart that was set free to start

the glittering ball she danced around
was once a broken mirror, a story unbound
but she transformed her fate, with a twirl and a spin
and her beauty shone so bright, her luck was rewritten within.

ghost of you

i search for connection, a heart that's true but i compared
every face with you
their eyes, a reminder of yours, so bright
their smile, a shadow of the one that lit up night

their laugh, a echo of the joy you brought
their touch, a whisper of the love we once had sought i try to
feel, to let go and be free
but your memory lingers, a ghost that haunts me

in every stranger, i see traces of you
a fleeting glimpse, a resemblance or two but like a mirage, it
vanishes in air
leaving me with longing, and a heart that's still not there

your presence still lingers, a shadow on my wall
a reminder of what I had, and what i've lost after all.

the biggest rebel

the heart, a traitor, betrays its own decree a slow surrender, a love letter to be
the head, a skeptic, struggles to comprehend as the heart, a rebel, chooses to love again.

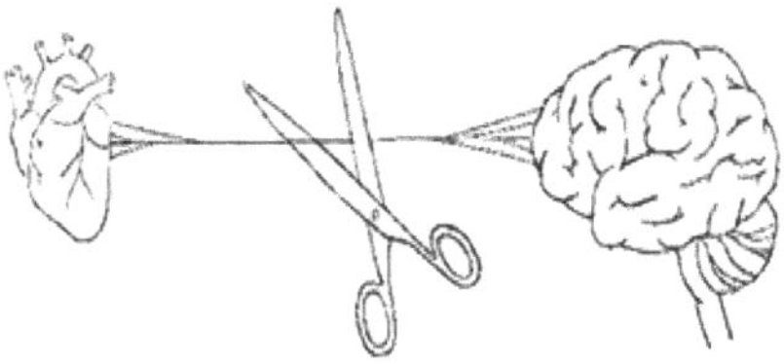

strength in the shadow

heavy heart, weighted soul
yet she stands, unbroken whole pain's dark depths, a hidden strength a resilience that defies length

rarely did tears trace her face
a smile, a shield, a hiding place
for the pain that threatened to consume a mask that hid the heart's deep wound

everything, yet nothing's worth left to feel the emptiness's chill
but still she rises, still she stands a survivor, in this shattered land

when hearts will align

my heart beats for one, i cannot disguise the truth that i long for her loving eyes
but though my soul yearns for her gentle grace i know my heart needs time to find its pace

i care for her more than words can say And so i'll wait, come what may
for love to bloom, for hearts to align
and when the time is right, our love will shine.

the sting of healing

unseen wounds, like hidden cuts, remain unfelt until a
stimulus brings the pain like hand sanitizer on a tender spot
a sudden sting, a hurt we hadn't noticed we got

healing's like that too, a gradual reveal
a process that exposes what we'd concealed a gentle touch, a
memory, a word, a sight
can bring to surface the pain we'd ignored in the night

but this is the first step to mend
facing the hurt, we begin to comprehend the parts of us that
still linger in the past and take the steps to heal, to forever last

winds gentle sway

i choose to kiss you in the wind's gentle sway,
the wind's soft touch is kinder than my lips' way.

i choose to hold you in my dreams so bright, in dreams, our
love shines on, without a fight.
i choose to love you in my heart's deepest place, in my heart,
our love will find its sacred space.

silent love

i choose to love you in silence true,
in silence, rejection's pain i flee from you. i choose to love you in loneliness too,
in loneliness, only i own you, that's true.
i choose to adore you from a distance wide, distance shields me from pain, my heart's inside.

persistence

i pushed on, not because it was easy to bear
but because i deserved to know i could face my fears my whole
being yearned to give up and rest
but i persisted, to prove i was worth the test

i kept going, though every part of me wanted to cease i rose
above, to discover my inner release
the strength to carry on, when all hope seemed to fade and in
that struggle, a resilient spirit was made

unspoken scars

your voice is free to speak the truth
about the pain they brought to your youth don't silence your words for their sake
their actions hurt, and your scars won't fake

now your story's yours to tell and share healing begins when secrets are spare

your voice voice is loud and clear your truth matters, banish all fear
you owe no loyalty to those who wronged your words will heal, and make you strong.

the storm survivor

you've weathered the tempests, and ridden out the gales
your heart has been tested, and your spirit has prevailed
you've seen the darkness, and faced the raging sea
and emerged stronger, with a soul that's wild and free

you've survived too many storms to be bothered by raindrops now
your strength is in your scars, and your beauty is in your brow.

turning blind

but we cannot simply sit and stare at our wounds forever
for in the stillness, our pain becomes a heavy feather
that weighs us down
the process, though painful and slow
requires us to be blind to our wounds, and let go.

eternal flame

my love for you will burn like the sun in the sky, enduring and bright, never to die.
as long as the moon illuminates the dark of night, my heart will beat for you, with a love so tight.

until the oceans' waves cease to crash and roar, and the tides of time run still, forevermore.
i'll love you until the end of time's sweet score, forever and always, my love for you will endure.

rewind your watch

when my final moment comes, and my heart beats no more
you can wind your watch, restart time's steady score
but know that in that moment, we were infinite and free
in the timeless space, where love was all that could be.
and in that eternal space, our love will still be found
where timelessness embraces us, in a love that's unbound
forever entwined, in a love that's infinite and profound.

clockless love

if you seek forever, i'll pull out the clock's heart so time stands still, and we never depart
in this moment, we'll be lost in love's sweet art where seconds fade, and our hearts never part

i'll whisper "i love you" with each tender breath with every smile, with every kiss, with every depth our love will be infinite, our moment will be vast in the stillness of time, our love will forever last

Honeyed light

your presence is a warm and golden glow like honeyed light, it shines and never fades a sweet serenity that my soul can know and in your eyes, my heart finds shady glades

with you, my worries lose their heavy weight like summer breeze, my fears are swept away the world's loud din and chaos cease to irritate and in your love, i find a peaceful stay

you are my Christmas joy, my new year's delight a love that's present, a love that's always bright
good things have been, good things are yet to come with you, my love, my heart is forever home.

soul flame

my love, i love you, without condition
no prerequisites, no ultimatums, no hesitation i love you as you are, and all you'll be
a love that's pure, and true, and eternal, you'll see

i loved you then, i love you now my love will last, forever somehow
through every up and down, every high and low my love will stand, unwavering, forever to grow

i'll be here when you need me, when you want me too but most of all, when your heart is feeling broken in two my love is godly, a prayer that's true
a vow that's unbreakable, a love that's always new

as they say, till death do us part
my love will shine, a beacon in your heart greater than all, it will forever be
a love that's eternal, a love that's meant to be.

star crossed hearts

you were a surprise, a moment so bright
a collision of stars, that shattered my night my world was neat,
but you sent it astray plummeting into the ocean, in a way

i never expected, it to be you i see
but now i'm certain, it's only you and me no looking back, our
paths have crossed
our hearts now entwined, like the stars that have lost

in your eyes, my world was rearranged
my heart now beats for you, my love now estranged from the
life i knew, before you came my way
now i'm forever changed, in every single way.

the kid in a candy aisle

like a siren's call, you beckon me a sweet temptation, hard to flee
my heart, aflutter, like a bird set free
craving the sweetness of your love, a bittersweet spree

i swore off love, like a vow to abstain
but your presence draws me in, like a sweet, sweet pain my resolve crumbles, like a fragile, hollow reed
i succumb to your charm, my heart's deepest need

the ache of our past, a wound still unhealed yet, i'd surrender all, my heart's fragile shield
to taste the sweetness of your love, one moment's delight and risk the agony, the darkness of night

my heart, a battlefield, where love and pain collide where the sweetness of your love, my soul cannot divide i'm lost in your eyes, a siren's call
forever bound, to the sweetness of your love, i'll fall.

“why should i love?”

our heart beats 100,000 times a day, give it a reason to beat, come what may. let love be the spark that ignites the fire, and passion be the fuel that never tires.

there’s serotonin in our body, true, give it a reason to flow, and see it shine through.
let joy be the sunshine that brightens our day, and laughter be the music that chases the blues away.

our lungs breathe in oxygen, a vital need, give them a reason to expand, and let life proceed.
let adventure be the wind that fills our sails, and exploration be the horizon that beckons us to set sail.

“why should i love?” II

our minds think thousands of thoughts, a never-ending stream,
give them a reason to wander, and let imagination beam.
let creativity be the brush that paints our dreams,
and innovation be the spark that makes our ideas gleam.

our souls yearn for connection, a deep human need,
give them a reason to reach out, and let love be the seed.
let empathy be the bridge that spans the gap, and
understanding be the language that speaks directly to the heart.

monsoon of love, rain of blood

in the rain, i stood and prayed
for my pain to wash away, like tears from my face i asked god
to mend my shattered soul
to make me stronger, to make me whole

i begged to quiet my mind's relentless pace to stop the
breaking, the constant ache
my heart can only take so much, i prayed
my lungs struggling to breathe, my eyes afraid

if i told you?

in secret, i'll love you from afar
my face unknown, my heart a scar
in darkest dreams, you shine so bright my guiding star, my beacon light

my mind is blank, my heart races fast in dreams, our love will forever last my soul is yours, in slumber i'll stay forever dreaming, night and day

but in real life, i'll remain unseen living in shadows, mystery my screen
from the darkness of my troubled mind i admire your light, so hard to find

you shine on mountains, deep in the sea illuminating all, including me
my heart dreams of you, both night and day forever in love, yet never to say

the tapestry that tears apart

in the tapestry of time, threads let loose the echoes of
yesterday slowly fade
a metamorphosis, like a sacred truce as i step into a future
unafraid

letting go, not an end but a start
i discover the dawn after the darkest night a healing journey of
the soul and heart
in the tender release of what's held tight

the ever-renovating home

people are rivers, ever flowing, ever go
you cannot make them homes, no matter how you try for they
will vanish, taking all you give, and leave you dry

like water, they will slip right through your hands ever
changing, shifting sands
you cannot grasp or hold them tight for they will flow away,
into the night

but fear not, for your home is not lost
it beats within your chest, a love that's been crossed look
inside yourself, and you will find
a heartbeat that's yours, a love that's truly divine

so let the rivers flow, and do not try to make them stay, or ask
them why
for your home is in your heart, a love so true and that, child, is
a home that's made for you.

him and i

for eternity, your beauty shines so bright things only i know, a secret delight
a mystery that holds me, in its sweet might your cover so fair, with title so grand
a story untold, that only i can stand every day, i read you, like a book unread
your pages so pure, with words yet unsaid your story unfolds, like a flower in bloom
a tale of wonder, that fills my heart with room

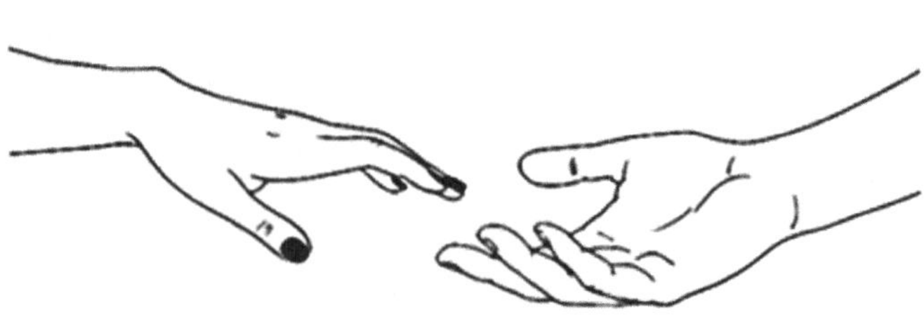

love at first word

you're my first, my love, like a twinkling star not just a first
kiss, or a first go far
but the first to make me feel complete
the first to show me love that's real and sweet

you're the first to make me feel like i'm enough to take my
heart and show me what it's made of you're the first to
whisper "i love you" in my ear and make me believe it, without
a single fear

with you, i've learned what love truly means
a love that's pure, and real, and not just a dream you're my
first, my love, my everything
forever and always, for you my heart will sing.

the winter sun

you were a surprise, a moment so bright
a collision of stars, that shattered my night my world was neat,
but you sent it astray plummeting into the ocean, in a way

i never expected, it to be you i see
But now i'm certain, it's only you and me no looking back, our
paths have crossed
our hearts now entwined, like the stars that have lost

in your eyes, my world was rearranged
my heart now beats for you, my love now estranged from the
life i knew, before you came my way
now i'm forever changed, in every single way.

always the poet, never the poetry

she had a library, full of stories untold
at first, she was afraid, her tales to unfold but he promised to stay, and read every one
the ones that were hers, the ones that had been undone

they sat on the shelves, collecting dust and pain abandoned by those who had broken her trust in vain some chapters seemed out of place, some words erased empty shelves where stories were taken, unseen and unembraced

but then a boy came, with a cart and a heart and filled it with her books, a brand new start
he dusted off the forgotten, and read through the night until he reached the bottom, and shone with delight

through the stacks, he wove a tale, a love so true but when he got up to leave, her heart broke anew
but he took her hand, and led her through the door to show her his library, and love her even more

he said he loved every word, every story she'd written
and he wasn't leaving her, but showing her his own vision a new library, full of tales, full of love and light
together they'd explore, through day and endless night.

ghost in your memory?

i thought immortality was promised in the hearts of those we
leave behind. yet, what if my whispers go unheard,
my footsteps fade into the quiet dusk?

do i not breathe in the memory of another, am i a ghost in a
living world,
a shadow cast without light,
an echo that never found a voice?

if no heart holds my story, no mind cradles my name,
am i a phantom, unseen and unfelt, already lost to the world's
amnesia?

in the stillness of forgotten dreams, i ponder my existence,
wondering if i ever truly lived, or if i was merely a fleeting sigh
in the breath of the universe.

eternal echoes

in the stillness of twilight, i hear her secrets told,
the wind whispers softly, of stories long and old.

she carries tales of lovers, parted by the sea,
their hearts bound by the breezes, whispering eternally.

she sings of ancient forests,
where trees once touched the sky, and echoes of their rustling
leaves, murmur as they sigh.

in her whispers, i find solace, in her breath, i find peace, the
wind and her whispers,
are where my soul finds release.

salt and stardust

in the ocean's deepest embrace, where salt meets the sky,
lie dreams woven in stardust, glistening from on high.

every grain of salt,
a tear shed in despair, every speck of stardust,
a wish whispered in the air.

they blend in the night,
where dreams and reality meet, salt and stardust,
make life's bittersweet.

we sail through salty seas, guided by stardust's glow,
navigating the tides of life, with hearts that ebb and flow.

the mosaic of my heart

shattered by life's cruelty, pieces scattered wide,
a heart left in fragments, nowhere left to hide.

yet from the broken pieces, a mosaic takes its form, every
shard a testament,
to weathering the storm.

in each colored fragment, lies a story of the past,
a heart's mosaic,
a beauty built to last.

with love and patient hands, it's mended whole again,
a mosaic of a heart,
stronger than it's ever been.

bloom & wither

in the garden of our days,
where moments bloom and fade, we watch the flowers blossom,
in sunshine and in shade.

with every petal's fall,
we witness life's brief span,
a cycle of bloom and wither, in the heart of man.

for every bloom that withers, another takes its place,
a reminder in the garden, of life's enduring grace.

so let us cherish blossoms, for soon they'll wither too,
in the dance of bloom and wither, life's beauty we pursue.

drifting in the shadows

drowning in my words, but outside i slip, through cracks i fade, losing my grip. people come and go like clouds in the sky, but i'm just a shadow, drifting by.

in crowded rooms, i feel so small, conversations rise, but i miss them all. always the last to catch on, it's true,
while my childhood walls cry out in blue.

can't escape the pull of my hometown, every visit, the dam breaks down.
hate's easier felt than the weight of blame, but what if it's me who holds the flames?

addicted to the fire

i get killed loving you, yet my heart returns, like a burned child,
drawn to the fire that burns.

your touch, a searing flame, but i crave it still,
for in your warmth, i find a thrill.

though ashes scatter, and scars remain,
a burned child loves the fire, despite the pain.

i know the danger, yet I don't retreat, for in loving you, even death is sweet

for the Hope of It All

to live for the hope of it all,
in the quiet of dawn's first light, where dreams and reality intertwine,
and the stars bow down to the rising sun, i find myself in the tender in-between,
a world where everything might be, if I dare to hold the fleeting hope, close enough to my heart to believe.

in the hush of a morning yet to bloom, i walk along paths of golden hues, where the whispers of the wind sing,
of stories that have yet to unfold, each step a promise of what could be, if only I let the light seep through,
the cracks in my soul, where doubt resides, and fear's shadow dances in the gloom.

i reach out to touch the sky,
fingers brushing against the edges of dreams, that hang like mist on a summer's morn, fading away with the warmth of the sun,
but oh, the joy in the reaching,
the thrill of believing in the unseen, for even if the dream should slip,
it leaves behind a trace of light.

● ● ● ● ●

to live for the hope of it all,
is to wander through the fields of possibility, where the wildflowers of wishes grow, untamed, in every color that hope knows,
it is to stand on the brink of the unknown, and leap with nothing but faith in your wings,
to fall, to rise, to try again,
for in the fall, new hope springs.

it is to find beauty in the journey, not in the destination alone,
to savor the taste of the 'almost',
to dance in the rhythm of 'not yet', for in every near miss, in every sigh, lies the heartbeat of hope,
a soft pulse, a gentle throb,
that reminds you why you keep on.

to live for the hope of it all,
is to paint your days in shades of maybe, to weave your nights with threads of someday,
and find in each moment, a glimpse, of the dreams that light your way,
it's the courage to love without knowing, to give without expecting return,
to embrace the fleeting with open arms, and find joy in the fleeting.

● ● ● ● ●

hope is the breath in your lungs,
the fire in your soul that refuses to dim, no matter how dark the night,
how long the road, how steep the climb, it's the voice that whispers,
in the silence of your doubt, that there's a reason to keep on,
to believe, to dream, to fight.
to live for the hope of it all,
is to find magic in the mundane,
to see the world through the eyes of a child, where every moment holds a secret,
A promise waiting to be revealed,
it's to carry the light of hope within you, even when the storm clouds gather,
and the winds of doubt howl loud

for in the end, hope is the anchor,
that keeps you grounded in the storm, it's the light that guides you home, when you've lost your way,
it's the reason you rise again,
after every fall, every tear, every sigh, for to live for the hope of it all,
is to truly live, to truly be alive.

does the butterfly get tired of flapping its wings?

i always wonder if the butterfly gets tired of flapping its wings
if the hummingbird feels monotony every time it sings
what if one morning, the sun did not want to rise? or if the moon decided to stop changing its size what if the cherry blossoms decide not to fall? what if the monsoons don't want to cry at all?
i wonder if the stars get tired, twinkling all night what if one day, even i want to give up this fight

in those eyes.

you could see things reflect in her eyes, your face, the water
and sometimes incomplete goodbyes
they were words staring into for days, but if you look long enough, you'd find reason for her silent ways
eyes are window to our soul
hers, were darker than the darkest hole they say the eyes never lie
is that why hers always cry?

in english you say "i love you" in poetry we say, if our love was a garden i wont let it die my dear. even if it means, watering it with my tears.

about the author

Saisha, a 15-year-old student at Vibgyor, is a multi-talented creative with a passion for writing, theatre, and design. Currently in grade 10, she has already made her mark as a rising storyteller. An accomplished writer, Saisha's poetry draws from her life experiences, capturing both the beauty and struggles she has encountered. Her book is a testament to those who have touched her life, offering words that rise from wounds, bandaged with love and wisdom. Beyond writing, Saisha is also skilled in video- making and editing, constantly exploring new ways to express her creativity.

Whether on stage, behind the camera, or with a pen in hand, Saisha's talent and determination continue to shine, making her a force to watch in the years to come.

"i really wish i could write like you." To write like me means to feel like me, you don't want that.